CLIMATE Change

The Vital Role of Deserts and Forests

CLIMATE Change

PROBLEMS and PROGRESS

CLIMATE Change
PROBLEMS and PROGRESS

The Vital Role of Deserts and Forests

James Shoals

Mason Crest

Mason Crest
450 Parkway Drive, Suite D
Broomall, PA 19008
www.masoncrest.com

© 2020 by Mason Crest, an imprint of National Highlights, Inc.

Printed and bound in the United States of America.

Series ISBN: 978-1-4222-4353-4
Hardback ISBN: 978-1-4222-4362-6
EBook ISBN: 978-1-4222-7457-6

First printing
1 3 5 7 9 8 6 4 2

Cover photographs by Dreamstime.com: Andrey Gudkov (left); Hpbphotos (right); Uros Ravbar (bottom); Nattama Dechangamjamras (bkgd.).

Library of Congress Cataloging-in-Publication Data is on file with the publisher.

QR Codes disclaimer:

CONTENTS

KEY ICONS TO LOOK FOR

Words to Understand: These words with their easy-to-understand definitions will increase the reader's understanding of the text, while building vocabulary skills.

Sidebars: This boxed material within the main text allows readers to build knowledge, gain insights, explore possibilities, and broaden their perspectives by weaving together additional information to provide realistic and holistic perspectives.

Educational Videos: Readers can view videos by scanning our QR codes, providing them with additional educational content to supplement the text. Examples include news coverage, moments in history, speeches, iconic moments, and much more!

Text-Dependent Questions: These questions send the reader back to the text for more careful attention to the evidence presented here.

Research Projects: Readers are pointed toward areas of further inquiry connected to each chapter. Suggestions are provided for projects that encourage deeper research and analysis.

Series Glossary of Key Terms: This back-of-the-book glossary contains terminology used through-out this series. Words found here increase the reader's ability to read and comprehend higher-level books and articles in this field.

canal irrigation a waterway that carries water from a body of water or source to the soil

combat to fight against something

combustion rapid oxidation accompanied by heat and light

degradation the act of degrading

endangered threatened with danger

exploitation selfish utilization

extinction dying out

grazing to munch on grassland

greenhouse effect an atmospheric heating process

infertile unproductive

inhabitant a person or an animal that inhabits a place, especially as a permanent resident

landslide downward sliding of a mass of soil

livelihood the means of supporting oneself, especially financially

monoculture the use of land for growing only one type of crop

pasture grass or other plants for feeding livestock

pesticide a chemical preparation for destroying plant pests

plantation a group of planted trees or plants

progressively change happening in stages

ranching an establishment maintained for raising livestock

sanitation protecting health, cleanliness

scarcity insufficiency of supply

shielding a person or a thing that protects

starvation the state of hunger

sustainable able to be maintained at a certain rate or level

timber wood prepared for use in building and carpentry

topsoil the upper part of the soil

vegetation all the plants of an area taken as a whole

INTRODUCTION

Today, deforestation and desertification are serious environmental issues. In recent years, they have caused a lot of damage all over the world. The earth's tropical rainforests are disappearing and drylands in arid and semiarid regions are degrading at a fast rate.

Deforestation and desertification reduce land's ability to support life. They degrade the whole ecosystem and disturb the environment throughout the world. Earlier, when developed countries urbanized their economy, it caused a lot of destruction to the natural environment. As a result, the world today is suffering from the scarcity of plants, animals, food, water, shelter, lifesaving medicines, fuel, and other basic necessities of life.

The main causes of deforestation and desertification are human activities and climate changes. In the future, deforestation and desertification will be among the greatest challenges to global economic growth. Efforts from all nations are required to deal with this pressing issue.

Forests

Forests are essential to sustain global ecosystems. They are important for plants, animals, and human beings as well. They cover 31 percent of the earth's land surface and are home to 80 percent of terrestrial and plant species. Due to deforestation, many plant and animal species are facing the threat of extinction.

The Forest Cycle

Forests go through cycles of growth and death, and in the process absorb and release carbon. They act as a carbon sink, a naturally occurring area where carbon dioxide is absorbed. Carbon dioxide is a greenhouse gas that traps the sun's heat and increases the global temperature. Tropical deforestation is accountable for about 20 percent of the world's carbon dioxide emissions each year. Rising temperatures lead to natural disasters. Therefore, forest plantation is essential to dealing with the effects of global warming.

Types of Forests

There are mainly three types of forests:

- Deciduous forests grow in places with mild winters and humid, wet summers. They are mainly found in Asia, Europe, Australia, New Zealand, North America, and South America.
- Coniferous forests grow in places with long, cold winters and cool, short summers. They are mainly found in East Asia, Canada, Europe, North America, and South America.
- Rainforests are home to almost 50 percent of the plant and animal species in the world. They grow in areas that experience heavy rainfall and steady sunlight. They are mainly found in parts of Africa, Southeast Asia, and parts of Central and South America.

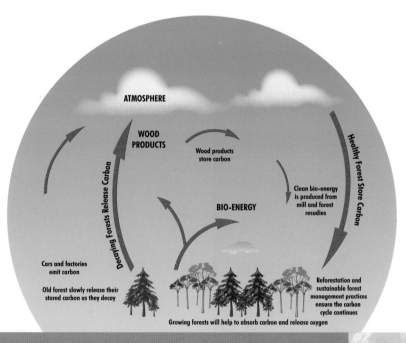

ATMOSPHERE

WOOD PRODUCTS

Wood products store carbon

Decaying Forests Release Carbon

Healthy Forest Store Carbon

BIO-ENERGY

Clean bio-energy is produced from mill and forest resudies

Cars and factories emit carbon

Old forest slowly release their stored carbon as they decay

Reforestation and sustainable forest management practices ensure the carbon cycle continues

Growing forests will help to absorb carbon and release oxygen

Climate Facts

- Around 1.6 billion people throughout the world depend on forests for their livelihoods.

- Around 30 million species of plants and animals are found in tropical rainforests.

Deforestation

Deforestation is the clearing of plants and trees to use the land for other purposes. Global deforestation began in 1960, and by the end of the nineteenth century, most of the world's dense forests were cleared. Since then, deforestation has been increasing at a high rate.

History

About 300 million years ago, the Carboniferous rain forests were destroyed due to climate change. This led to the death of many hundreds of plants and animals species. The change in climate was sudden and affected large groups of amphibians and reptiles. Since then the rain forests have been continuously shrinking.

Global Deforestation

Rapid population growth and poverty has increased the demand for farming, grazing cattle, plantation of commodities, urbanization, and the growth of industries. These activities contribute to global deforestation.

Growing Urbanization

Urbanization is still leading to deforestation in many parts of the world. Almost 30 percent of the world's rain forests are located in Brazil. At present, Brazil has the highest annual rate of deforestation. About 90 to 95 percent of the rain forests in the Atlantic coast of Brazil have been deforested. Scientists believe that if this trend persists, it may have severe effects on the worldwide climate and environment.

Deforestation basics: National Geographic

Climate Facts

- Tropical rain forests used to cover 14 percent of the earth's surface. However, due to deforestation, now they only cover 6 percent of the land surface.
- On average, about 11,600 square yards (9,712 sq. m) of earth's forests are cleared every second.

Causes of Deforestation

For thousands of years people have been clearing land for growing crops and raising livestock. As civilizations grew, urbanization and industrialization increased. Now, people clear not only land for cultivation, but also cut down forests to build roads, industries, and cities.

Development of Infrastructure

Human beings have come a long way since the age of hunter-gatherers. However, in doing so we have caused immense loss to the planet. Every day millions of people around the world are traveling from one place to another by trains, buses, and cars. Have you ever wondered how many acres of land have been cleared to connect these places?

Food Requirements

To meet the growing demands of food, millions of acres of forested land across the world has been converted to agricultural land and **pastures**. Forested areas are being opened up for migratory farmers, who move in and clear the land, usually by burning down the trees. Apart from growing crops, many farmers also clear land to rear livestock. The increase in global demand for meat has greatly increased the demand for cattle grazing. In Brazil, cattle grazing is responsible for about 80 percent of rainforest destruction.

Subsistence Farming

Poverty is often seen as one of the reasons for deforestation. In many places around the world, farmers practice subsistence farming. This means growing food crops to meet the food requirements of one's own family. In many places around the world, forested hillsides have been converted to subsistence farming plots.

Climate Facts

- About 50 percent of the world's forests are under the threat of being cleared for farming.

- According to the Food and Agriculture Organization of the United Nations (FAO), an estimated 4,600 sq. miles (12,000 sq. km) of rainforest area was cut down between 2004 and 2005 due to soybean expansion.

Lumber Industry

The demand for timber has risen sharply since the Industrial Revolution. Although coal was mined in the seventeenth century, timber acted as a primary source of fuel for many industries. Thus as the number of industries grew, large areas became barren. Many industries still use wood to produce energy. In fact, most logged trees are used for energy production.

Paper Production

Wood pulp is used for making paper. Every year, giant paper producers in the world are cutting down forests for paper production. Almost 35 percent of the trees cut worldwide are used for paper production. However, in recent years, paper industrialists are moving toward sustainable production that includes recycling paper.

Furniture and Construction

The ever-increasing demand for wooden furniture is one of the driving forces behind massive deforestation around the world. Timber is also used in the construction of buildings and in flooring. Every year, thousands of acres of tropical forests are being cleared to meet these requirements.

Illegal Logging

Most tree logging around the world is illegal. Weak enforcement of laws by governments as well as corporate greed have encouraged the growth of illegal timber gangs. The Congo Basin in Africa and the Amazon rainforests are facing the gravest threats from illegal logging.

Illegal logging in Africa

Climate Facts

• In Indonesia, 73 percent of logging is illegal, while in Brazil 80 percent of logging is illegal.

• The United States is the largest producer and consumer of timber.

Climate Change & Forests

orests play a very important role in balancing the water cycle. Disturbing the earth's water cycle leads to climate change, which affects food production, water supplies, health, and the well-being of humans.

Water Cycle

Deforestation does not allow water to recycle in the forest ecosystem. This leads to reduction in the precipitation level and to a drier climate. Low levels of rainfall can affect the basic needs of humans, such as the availability of drinking water, water for irrigation, etc. This could even lead to the **extinction** of some species.

Irregular Rainfall

Though the major impact of deforestation on precipitation is observed in and near the deforested regions, it also influences rainfall in the mid and high latitudes. Hence, deforestation in the Amazon Basin affects rainfall from Mexico to Texas, while deforestation in Southeast Asia is responsible for changing the rainfall patterns in China and the Balkan Peninsula.

Warming of Earth

Forests form a **shielding** layer that prevents the sun's rays from reaching the earth's surface. However, when trees are cut down, the earth's surface is exposed to solar radiation. Such exposure makes the earth warm, which eventually warms the air above. This is how the climate becomes drier and global temperatures increase. Global warming and changes in the climate patterns are a result of this development.

Climate Facts

● Around 125,000 years ago, the sea level was about 18 feet (5.4 m) higher as compared to the current sea level.

● In the 1990s, approximately 600,000 deaths occurred worldwide due to climate-related natural disasters.

Biodiversity Disaster

Biodiversity refers to the different species and the variety of life forms found on earth. It contributes to the health and well-being of humans. Deforestation interrupts the ecosystem and ultimately leads to the loss of biodiversity.

Disappearing Animals

The removal of trees destroys the habitats and the food sources available in the forests. One of the animals under threat is the African elephant. In the early part of the twentieth century, there may have been as many as three to five million African elephants; now, there are around 415,000.

Mass Extinctions

A recent study predicts that by the end of the twenty-first century, more than 40 percent of the plant and animal species in Southeast Asia could face mass extinction. Up to 75 percent of the earth's reef-building corals are in danger of extinction. If the temperature throughout the world rises by 6.5°F (3.5°C), up to 70 percent of the well-known species may become extinct.

Saving the white rhino

Climate Facts

● Only 1 percent of the plant species in rainforests have been tested for their medical value.

● Tropical rainforests have the largest extinction rate of species.

Deforestation in China

China became one of the world's leading timber exporters in the mid-1990s. Today, deforestation is a major issue in China. Commercial logging is the key reason leading to the rapid destruction of Chinese forests. However, China has begun reforestation practices to deal with this issue.

Ban on Logging

During the last two decades, almost 50 percent of the forests in northern and central China have been deforested to meet the demand of wood and **timber**. In 1999, the Chinese government banned logging in forests and imposed a tax on wooden flooring. This resulted in massive import of wood by China. This demand was met through illegal logging and deforestation in other regions such as Siberia, Brazil, and Indonesia.

The Great Green Wall

The people and the government of China are making reforestation efforts. The Great Green Wall project, which began in 1978, made it compulsory for every citizen above the age of eleven to plant at least three saplings every year. Over the last decade, Chinese citizens have planted around fifty-six billion trees across the country.

Illegal Logging on the Rise

The growing demand for wood in China encouraged illegal logging in many countries such as Madagascar, Indonesia, and the Philippines. Huge amounts of illegal tropical rainforest timber from Indonesia, rosewood from Madagascar, and tree trunks from the Philippines were exported to China.

Climate Facts

- Forests cover 14 percent of total Chinese land.

- Every year, around 1,930 sq. miles (5,000 sq. km) of forests are destroyed by illegal logging and the burning of agricultural land.

Palm Oil Cultivation

Palm oil **plantations** have grown **progressively** in recent years. Palm oil is an eco-friendly fuel and a cost-effective substitute to other vegetable oils. It is a healthy food item and is easily produced. About 87 percent of the world's palm oil is produced in Malaysia and Indonesia.

Environmental Impact

Over the past two decades, the rainforests of Southeast Asia have been rapidly cleared for palm oil cultivation, leading to global warming, drought, **landslide**, air and water pollution, desertification, and loss of soil nutrients and biodiversity. Palm oil cultivation is one of the leading causes of deforestation in Southeast Asia. Around 2.3 million square yards (2 million sq m) of area are destroyed every hour by burning.

Impact on Biodiversity

These rainforests are home to around twenty thousand flowering plant species, three thousand tree species, three hundred thousand animal species, and thousands of other unknown species. Clearing these forests for palm oil has resulted in the loss of habitat for these animals. The most affected animal is the orangutan. There are only sixty thousand orangutans left on the Indonesian islands of Sumatra and Borneo.

Impact on Human Life

Deforestation due to palm plantations has led to massive climate pollution throughout the world. Palm oil cultivation is harming the physical well-being and livelihoods of the local **inhabitants** of Southeast Asia. In 2011, a landslide in Thailand killed around forty people. Researchers believe that the landslide occurred due to palm oil cultivation in that area.

Climate Facts

- Palm oil cultivation has become a threat to both the local and global surroundings of Southeast Asia.

- Burning of forests for palm oil cultivation is accountable for 15 percent of global carbon emissions.

Amazon Rainforests

The Amazon rainforest, also known as the "Lungs of our Planet," is the world's largest tropical rainforest. It accounts for 1.4 billion acres of land and produces almost 20 percent of the world's oxygen. The rainforest covers about half of Brazil, large areas of Columbia, Venezuela, and the eastern regions of Peru.

Deforestation

About 47 percent of the Amazon rainforest has been deforested. Since the 1990s, deforestation in the Amazon region has continued to increase annually. In comparison to 1992, deforestation rose by 32 percent in 1996. In 2000–05, it rose by 18 percent in comparison to the previous five years. By 2018, the acreage lost was about a quarter of the high level set in 2004.

Causes

Deforestation in the Amazon rainforest is caused by cattle grazing, large-scale farming of soybeans, and the construction of property. Cattle **ranching** resulted in 60–70 percent of the deforestation in Amazonia.

Effects

The **exploitation** of the Amazon rainforest has severely affected the physical and social life of the local people. Since the 1990s, more than ninety tribes have been destroyed, leaving only 200,000 people out of a population of 10 million in the Amazonia, about 500 years ago. The removal of forests is also responsible for greenhouse gas emissions, loss of biodiversity, global warming, and the release of vast amounts of CO_2 into the atmosphere, along with water and air pollution, flooding, and soil erosion.

Climate Facts

- The area covered by the Amazon rainforest is sufficient to make a new country.

- Around 10 percent of the world's known species of animals live in the Amazon rainforest

Deforestation in Madagascar

Madagascar is the fourth largest island in the world and is one of the world's poorest countries. More than 90 percent of the original forests have been destroyed since humans entered the island about two thousand years ago. French rule in 1895 led to the destruction of almost 70 percent of the forest cover.

Effects

Due to massive deforestation in Madagascar, the island is unable to produce and supply sufficient food, shelter, fresh water, and **sanitation** facilities to its growing population. The impact of deforestation in this area has led to global warming, diminishing biodiversity, soil erosion, and desertification.

Soil Erosion

Due to massive deforestation, many parts of Madagascar are suffering from soil erosion. The removal of trees resulted in erosion of the nutrient-rich **topsoil**, leaving most of the land infertile. About four hundred tons of soil per 10,000 sq. m is lost to erosion every year, polluting the neighboring Indian Ocean.

Animal Extinction

The destruction of these forests has **endangered** a large number of insects, tortoises, giant predatory raptors, giant lemurs, hippopotamuses, and other megafauna living in the island. At least seventeen species of the giant lemur, and almost all large animal species, have gone extinct. The silky sifaka, one of the rarest mammals, is found in the forests of Madagascar. This lemur has been brought to the verge of extinction due to deforestation.

Climate Facts

- The introduction of coffee as a cash crop during the French rule is a major cause of deforestation in Madagascar.

- Since the time humans stepped on the island of Madagascar, at least seventeen species of the giant lemur have gone extinct.

Desertification

The **degradation** of dry lands is known as desertification. The soil becomes dry and is unable to support **vegetation**. Desertification is a fast process and can convert dry lands into deserts over a few seasons.

Drylands

Drylands are delicate environments that experience little, irregular rainfall throughout the year. As a result, the water availability in such areas is insufficient. Desertification affects the **livelihood** of millions of people who depend on the drylands for farming and other activities.

Danger to Crop Cultivation

Drylands are home to the rich biodiversity of the world. Some of the most important food grains like corn, wheat, rice, and millet are grown in these areas. More than 30 percent of the crops consumed worldwide are cultivated in drylands. About 10 to 20 percent of the earth's drylands have already been destroyed and more than a billion people are in danger from future desertification.

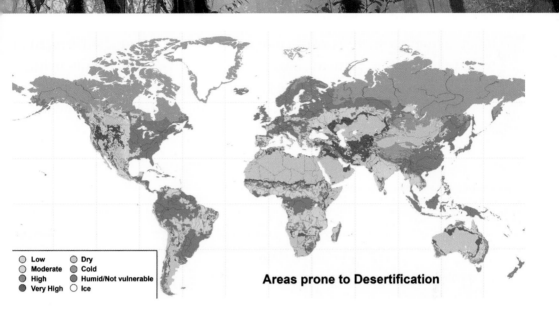

Low
Moderate
High
Very High
Dry
Cold
Humid/Not vulnerable
Ice

Areas prone to Desertification

Coverage

Drylands that are destroyed by desertification are mainly located in the arid, semiarid, and subhumid parts of the world. They cover up to 40 percent of the earth's land surface. About 50 percent of the countries worldwide have parts or their entire lands covered in dryland environments. Approximately 25 percent of the world's land has already been affected by desertification.

Climate Facts

• The drylands of about one hundred ten countries are at risk of desertification.

• One-fifth of the world's population lives in drylands.

Causes of Desertification

Human activities such as over-cultivation, poor farming, bad irrigation techniques, and overgrazing have reduced the biological productivity of drylands and have led to climate change, global warming, and the **greenhouse effect**. This complex relationship between the natural environment and human activities is promoting desertification.

Over-cultivation

The rapidly growing population is one of the reasons why farmers have been over-cultivating land. Growing too many crops for years on the same piece of land makes the soil less fertile and less productive. This damages the soil structure and with time, the over-cultivated land becomes desertified.

Overgrazing

Excessive **grazing** by animals can wipe out the vegetation of grasslands, leading to soil erosion and desertification. In the past, humans used to move their livestock depending on the food and water availability. This movement became restricted once humans began to settle down in places with a steady food supply. As a result, continuous grazing of the same land by livestock has contributed to desertification.

Poor Farming Methods

Monoculture, intensive agriculture, **canal irrigation**, and the use of **pesticides** prevent plant growth and lead to desertification. In 2010, a major drought in the Sahel region had put millions of people in immediate danger of **starvation**. The drought was primarily caused by over-cultivation, overgrazing, and poor farming and irrigation practices.

The vast majority of this cleared land is used for one purpose alone

Overgrazing effects on forests

Climate Facts

• Each year, about five million tons of pesticides are used worldwide for agricultural purposes.

• Around 70 percent of the arid land has already been desertified due to poor farming and irrigation techniques.

esertification is caused by both natural causes and human activities. Natural causes may include climate changes and natural disasters, such as droughts, hurricanes, and floods. These causes may change with time, or the locations may vary, but ultimately they reduce land productivity and cause land degradation.

Climate Change

Human activities, such as **combustion** of fossil fuels, have increased the levels of greenhouse gases in the atmosphere. Over the past one hundred years, the greenhouse effect has increased global temperatures by 0.3°C to 0.6°C. This has brought about major changes in the earth's climate. The changing rainfall patterns in many areas lead to damaging droughts, floods, and desertification.

Droughts

Drought is a phase of dry weather caused by the lack of rainfall for a long period in an area. The shortage of water results in the degradation of natural vegetation and affects plants, animals, and people. The threat of drought may also lead to human activities such as overgrazing and over-cultivation. During 1960–80, the Sahel region suffered from a severe period of drought, killing almost 100,00 people.

Mining

Mining is one of the leading causes of land degradation around the world. Mining may happen at the surface or under the ground. Surface mining leads to immediate degradation of the land area. It begins with the removal of all vegetation from the area. The miners scrape off the top layer of soil to extract the precious minerals, which causes the soil to lose its fertility.

Climate Facts

• Around 3.4 billion acres (1.4 billion hectares) of land in Asia have been affected by desertification.

• Every year, abut 29 million acres (12 million hectares) of land worldwide is lost to degradation.

Impact of Desertification

Desertification is known to have adverse environmental, social, and physical impacts. It reduces the capacity of land to sustain life, which in turn directly affects plants, livestock, agricultural crops, people, and the developing countries of the world.

Environmental Impact

Desertification makes the soil dry and **infertile**. The loss of nutritive value no longer allows the soil to support plant and animal life. Land degradation can have serious effects on the water cycle and the environment. It leads to soil erosion, water erosion, landslides, droughts, dust storms, soil acidification, soil pollution, water pollution, and increased salinity.

Social Impact

Desertification and land degradation leads the rural population to abandon farming and migrate to urban areas in search of new opportunities. The increase of people in urban areas has resulted in overpopulation and food insecurity. This is the reason why food production is also suffering. In just over twenty years, around 10 million people in Africa have migrated to cities in search of a healthier life.

Physical Impact

Desertification affects approximately 1.2 billion people worldwide. Land degradation leads to poverty, the loss of vegetation, and emigration. It threatens the production and supply of food and human well-being. Today, in the Sahel region, more than eighteen million people are affected by hunger and around one million children are at risk of malnutrition.

Climate Facts

- Desertification causes a loss of $45 billion in global incomes every year.

- Every year, approximately 3 million acres (12 million hectares) of land become useless due to desertification.

Ecosystem and Biodiversity

Ecosystem refers to the plants and animals living in a particular area that are dependent on each other and their surroundings. Thus, if any one element of the ecosystem is affected, the whole ecosystem is bound to suffer. The destruction of ecosystems over time leads to the loss of global biodiversity.

Damaged Ecosystems

The animals and plant species from the drylands are very well adapted to the extreme and harsh environment. Drought, over exploitation of land, and salinity destroy the soil, the habitats, and sources of food and water. Animals, trees, and other plants can no longer grow in a damaged ecosystem.

Plant Biodiversity

Desertification has reduced about 12.5 percent of the world's plant biodiversity. Changing climate, global warming, and the loss of habitats and animal species are all impacts of the reduction in plant biodiversity. Thus, in order to preserve the ecosystem, it is essential to maintain the rich plant biodiversity of earth.

Animal Biodiversity

Desertification leads to habitat degradation and loss of food sources for animals. This affects their breeding and mating cycles, leading to fewer births and the loss of animal biodiversity. Animals without food, shelter, and protection are at a risk of extinction. In the twentieth century, urbanization and poor farming in Spain destroyed the habitat of the Iberian lynx, reducing their population to a mere one hundred.

Climate Facts

- Due to the effects of climate change, species are dying one hundred to one thousand times faster than the natural rate.

- Around 4,500 known species in the United States alone are at risk of extinction.

Desertification in China

Desertification is a huge environmental problem in China. Around 28 percent of the total area in China is either enclosed by desert or is territory suffering from desertification. More than 70 percent of the land degradation in China is happening in the north, northwest, and northeast of China.

Human Contribution

In addition to climate change, human activities are also a major contributor to desertification in China. A rapid increase in population has led to the overutilization of land resources, including intensification of agricultural activities and animal husbandry. Mining, tourism, and city building are other activities that have led to land degradation in China.

Dust Storms

Extreme droughts have had major environmental impacts in Beijing, the capital of China. Strong winds often carry soil from northwest drylands, which travel hundreds of miles to China's eastern regions, forming huge dust clouds. Over the past two decades, dust storms have become an annual problem in Beijing.

Effects of Dust Clouds

Dust clouds are thick and choking and may cause breathing difficulties, asthma attacks, and allergic reactions if inhaled. When the wind blows in spring, people have to wear masks and there is reduced visibility on roads. As a result, traffic slows down, flights have to be canceled, and airports are closed.

Climate Facts

- Scientists have estimated that each year around 1,150 sq. miles (3000 sq km) of arable land in China become desertified.

- About 60 percent of the total Chinese population lives in desertified areas.

Desertification in Africa

Desertification has had the greatest impact in Africa. Two-thirds of African land is covered by deserts and drylands, of which 27 percent is already degraded. In recent years, the rate of food production and crop yields in many parts of Africa has quickly declined.

South Africa

About 50 percent of Southern Africa is covered by semiarid land. Due to human activities, this area now has desert-like conditions. Today, around 30 percent of the South African land is severely degraded and the rest faces the threat of desertification.

Impact on Human Life

Since 2001, consecutive droughts in South Africa have posed serious threats to the livelihoods of millions of people. In 2002–03, a food deficit of around 3.3 million tons was recorded, which affected almost 14.4 million people. The degraded land can no longer be used for crop production or feeding livestock.

Lake Chad

Since 2001, consecutive droughts in South Africa have caused severe problems. In the last forty years, Lake Chad, one of Africa's largest freshwater lakes, has shrunk to one-twelfth of its size. In 1963, the lake enclosed around 9,600 sq. miles (25,000 sq km) of area, which has shrunk by 95 percent. Researchers believe that the drying of wet areas in Chad is a result of human activities, and that the lake will evaporate completely over the next twenty years if efforts to prevent this are not made.

Climate Facts

• Around 65 percent of the total African population is affected by desertification.

• Farm yields across Africa are only one-third of those achieved by their Asian counterparts.

Sustainable Practices

Our earth can no longer bear the pressure of human demands. It is time for people and nations to unite and find solutions to turn around the global threat. We need to adopt **sustainable** forestry practices to maintain our forests, so that we are able to meet the challenges of climate change.

Sustainable Forestry

The employment of unsustainable practices in the Amazon rainforest has already degraded more than one-third of the forestry land. Sustainable methods of agriculture should be employed to deal with the problem. Farmers must practice processes such as agroforestry (farming that involves cultivation of trees) and intercropping.

Reforestation

Governments and citizens together must take steps to increase the forestry land on earth. Over the last two decades, China's reforestation and tree planting program has increased its forest cover from 12 percent to 16.55 percent. In the last few years, many East Asian countries have increased their forest cover by practicing reforestation and afforestation.

How Can I Contribute?

Each of us can contribute to saving the planet from destruction. Reduce the consumption of paper products, avoid wasting paper, switch to paperless billing, and recycle and reuse paper whenever possible. Look for a reliable logo while buying products and always purchase from sustainable manufacturers. Plant trees and learn how to take care of plants and soil.

Climate Facts

- World Forestry Day is celebrated on March 21.

- June 17 is globally renowned as the World Day to Combat Desertification and Drought.

1. What is a carbon sink?

2. Name some of the ways that people are using timber in increasing ways.

3. What is the Green Great Wall?

4. What countries are being greatly harmed by palm oil overcultivation?

5. What nickname does the text give for the Amazon rainforest?

6. On what island does the threatened silky siafa live?

7. Along with climate change, name one of the key factors the text cites for increased desertification.

8. What African lake does the text describe as shrinking massively in recent years?

1. Do some research on where a particular paper product you use is made—notebook paper, paper towels, textbooks, etc. Where is the paper sourced from? Could you choose another source that was more forest-friendly?

2. Reducing paper use is one way to reduce deforestation. Make a chart of 10 ways that you or your family or class could work toward reducing paper use in your lives.

3. Palm oil, as the text shows, is almost directly responsible for massive deforestation. Many companies have promised to reduce their use of the oil. Research some of these and find out what steps the companies took. Can you add some of these products to your daily use?

FIND OUT MORE

Books

Horning, Nadia Rabesahala. *The Politics of Deforestation in Africa: Madagascar, Tanzania, and Uganda.* New York: Palgrave Macmillan, 2018.

Rees, Paul A. *Examining Ecology: Exercises in Environmental Biology and Conservation.* San Diego: Academic Press, 2017.

Surui BS, Almir Narayamoga and Corine Sambrun. *Save the Planet: An Amazonian Tribal Leader Fights for His People, the Rainforest, and the Earth.* Tucson, AZ: Schaffner Press, 2018.

On the Internet

International Union of Concerned Scientists
www.iucn.org/resources/issues-briefs/deforestation-and-forest-degradation

National Geographic on deforestation
www.nationalgeographic.com/environment/global-warming/deforestation/

World Wildlife Fund on deforestation
www.worldwildlife.org/threats/deforestation-and-forest-degradation

bioaccumulation the process of the buildup of toxic chemical substances in the body

biodiversity the diversity of plant and animal life in a habitat (or in the world as a whole)

ecosystem refers to a community of organisms, their interaction with each other, and their physical environment

famine a severe shortage of food (as through crop failure), resulting in hunger, starvation, and death

hydrophobic tending to repel, and not absorb water or become wet by water

irrigation the method of providing water to agricultural fields

La Niña periodic, significant cooling of the surface waters of the equatorial Pacific Ocean, which causes abnormal weather patterns

migration the movement of persons or animals from one country or locality to another

pollutants the foreign materials which are harmful to the environment

precipitation the falling to earth of any form of water (rain, snow, hail, sleet, or mist)

stressors processes or events that cause stress

susceptible yielding readily to or capable of

symbiotic the interaction between organisms (especially of different species) that live together and happen to benefit from each other

vulnerable someone or something that can be easily harmed or attacked

INDEX

Photo Credits